4/21/15

COOL STUFF to SEW

Stephanie Turnbull

A⁺
Smart Apple Media

Published by Smart Apple Media, an imprint of Black Rabbit Books
P.O. Box 3263, Mankato, Minnesota 56002
www.blackrabbitbooks.com

Designed and illustrated by Guy Callaby
Edited by Mary-Jane Wilkins

Library of Congress Cataloging-in-Publication Data

Turnbull, Stephanie, author.
Cool stuff to sew / Stephanie Turnbull.
    pages cm. -- (Cool stuff)
Audience: Grade 4 to 6.
Includes index.
ISBN 978-1-62588-191-5
1. Sewing--Juvenile literature. 2. Handicraft--Juvenile literature. I.
Title.
TT712.T87 2015
646.2--dc23

                          2013050751

Picture credits
t = top, b = bottom, l = left, r = right, c = center
page 1 windu, 2-3 Zhukov Oleg; 4t OtnaYdur, c Elnur;
5c MARGRIT HIRSCH, b Africa Studio; 6tl Lubava, tc tehcheesiong,
b Birute Vijeikiene; 7 Suslik1983; 8t Louella938/all Shutterstock,
b Mim Waller; 9c Liufuyu/Thinkstock, b MARGRIT HIRSCH/
Shutterstock, 10 and 11 Mim Waller; 12l Dancing Fish/Shutterstock,
r Mim Waller; 13 Mim Waller; 14tr Madlen/Shutterstock; c Mim
Waller, b photokup/Shutterstock; 15s and c Mim Waller, b zhu
difeng; 16t Sergey Novikov/both Shutterstock; 17 Mim Waller;
18t Birute Vijeikiene/Shutterstock, b Mim Waller; 19 Mim Waller;
20 Ljupco Smokovski/Shutterstock; 21 Mim Waller; 22t Shebeko,
tl F. JIMENEZ MECA, b Mim Waller; 23, 24, 25t Mim Waller,
b Africa Studio; 26t Roman Pyshchyk/both Shutterstock,
b Mim Waller; 27t Mim Waller, b kuleczka; 28t keantian/both
Shutterstock, r Mim Waller, b Chimpinski; 29t mark higgins/
Shutterstock, b Mim Waller; 3ot LooksLikeLisa, b Birute Vijeikiene;
31 SisterF/all Shutterstock
lightbulb in Cool Ideas boxes Designs Stock/Shutterstock
Cover background Jupiterimages/Thinkstock, small images
Mim Waller

Printed in the United States of America
at Corporate Graphics, North Mankato, Minnesota
PO: DAD0058c
PO Date: 032015

9 8 7 6 5 4 3

Contents

Start Sewing!

Sewing is a really cool craft. It's not expensive or difficult to do, and with just a few easy stitches and some basic materials, you can create fantastic games, toys, bags, cards, and much more.

Good sewing kits include all kinds of useful items, such as scissors, pins, needles, buttons, and thread.

Did You Know?

The skill of sewing by hand goes back to prehistoric times, when people made fur and skin clothes using bone needles and thread from stringy animal sinews.

Hand Sewing

Sewing machines are great time-saving devices for putting together complicated clothes, but it's best to learn to hand sew first. None of the projects in this book needs a sewing machine—just a needle, thread, and some fabric.

Clever Crafts

Sewing is handy for everyday tasks such as mending clothes, but it can also be amazingly creative. Skilled artists sew intricate **embroideries**, patchwork quilts, and wall hangings. Other sewing experts design and produce unique hand-made shoes, hats, and furniture.

Quilters sew shaped pieces of fabric together. Then they stitch on thick backing layers of fabric.

Cool Idea

Sewing equipment is small and easy to lose, so keep needles in cases and pins in pin cushions. Store thread neatly in a bin or box, so it doesn't get in a tangle!

Start with the simple projects in this book, and who knows—one day you might be a famous fashion designer, craft expert, or artist!

Needles and Thread

The first step in learning to sew is to find a needle! Ordinary sewing needles are straight and sharp-ended. They vary in size according to the thickness of your thread and fabric.

Steady Threading

Cut a length of thread: not so short that you can only sew a few stitches, but not so long that it gets tangled. A piece the length of your arm is about right. Now feed it through the needle's eye (hole), and tie a knot. Sit in a well-lit place so you can see what you're doing.

1. *Snip the top of the thread at an angle to make a neat point. It's hard to push a ragged end through the eye. Or you could wet it in your mouth to create a flatter tip.*

2. *Hold the needle between your thumb and first finger, with the eye facing you. Pick up the end of the thread with your other thumb and first finger and feed it through the eye.*

Cool Idea

*If you have a sewing kit, it may include a **threader**. Push the wire loop through the needle's eye, feed the thread through the loop, and pull it back through the eye. Just like that— a threaded needle!*

3. *Pull at least 6 inches (15 cm) of thread through the eye, or it may fall out again. Now stick the needle safely into a pin cushion while you tie the knot at the end of the thread.*

4. *Take the end in one hand, and use your free hand to wrap it twice around your first finger. Hold it in place with your thumb.*

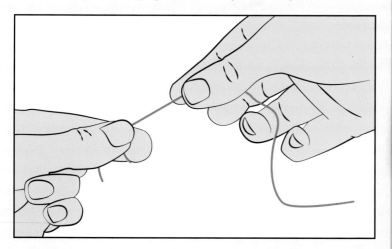

5. *Use your thumb to roll the loop slowly off your finger.*

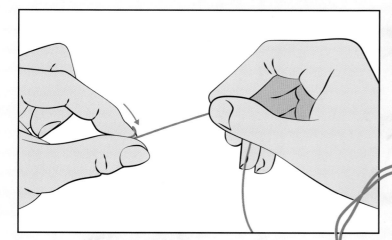

6. *Now trap it and push it back with the tip of your middle finger, so it forms a knot.*

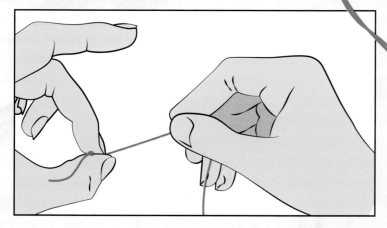

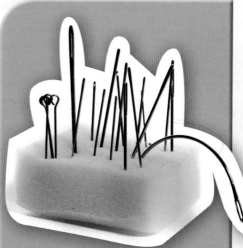

Did You Know?

Embroidery needles have an extra-long eye for thick thread. **Darning** *needles are fat and blunt for pushing through thick material, and some needles are curved for reaching awkward angles.*

Single or Double?

Sewing with a single thread is good when you want stitches to be thin and hidden. If you make a mistake, it's easy to unthread the needle, rip stitches, and thread it again.

For thicker, stronger stitches, use a double thread. This means pulling the thread further in step 3, and then looping and rolling both ends together in steps 4 and 5.

Simple Stitches

You only need a few stitches to start with. Follow these easy steps to learn three basic (but very useful) stitches. Find a scrap of fabric to practice them on, making sure not to pull the stitches too tight.

Running Stitch

This is probably the easiest stitch of all.

1. Push your needle up through the fabric, so the knot is on the back. Now push the needle back through, and up again, in the line where you want to stitch.

2. Pull the needle through so the thread is tight. You've made your first stitch!

3. Continue in the same way to the end of the line. Try to keep the stitches the same size.

4. To finish, push your needle through to the back on the last stitch and turn over the fabric. On the back, feed the thread under the last stitch, and pull it through until just a small loop of thread is loose.

5. Feed the needle through the loop, and pull it tight to make a knot. Cut off the thread.

Don't wait until your thread is really short, otherwise you won't have enough to make a knot!

 **Cool Idea** *Try lacing a contrasting color thread in and out of running stitches to make a wiggly effect.*

Backstitch

Backstitch is like running stitch, but you keep going back to fill in gaps between stitches. It creates a neat, unbroken line. Start with steps 1 and 2 of running stitch, and then poke the needle back through the fabric at the end of the first stitch.

Push the needle back up a space away from the stitch, and then pull through the thread. Repeat to fill the line.

Running stitch runs up and down through the material like this...

...but backstitch loops back each time like this.

Up-and-Over Stitch

To sew two pieces of fabric together, start by pushing the needle up through the top layer of fabric, so the knot will be hidden in the middle.

Then feed the needle and thread up from the bottom layer, out of the top layer, then back round to the bottom layer again. Repeat all the way along.

Did You Know?

Cross-stitch is a traditional style of sewing that has been used for hundreds of years to embroider patterns and pictures.

Fantastic Felt

Felt is the perfect fabric for sewing. It comes in bright colors, is easy to cut, and doesn't **fray**. Here are two cool felt craft projects to try. They're ideal for practicing the three types of stitches from pages 8 and 9.

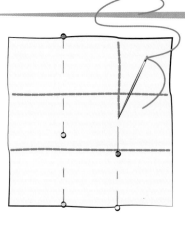

Tic Tac Toe

This fun felt board game is really quick and easy to make. Why not give it to someone as a gift?

1. *Cut a 6 inches (15 cm) square of felt in any color. Using a ruler and pins, mark two vertical lines and two horizontal lines, each 2 inches (5 cm) apart.*

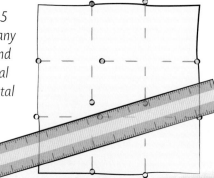

2. *Sew along each line in brightly-colored thread, removing each pin as you come to it.*

3. *On a different colored felt piece, draw around something circular, such as a bottle top, and cut out five circles. Decorate them with stitching if you like.*

4. *Cut ten strips in another color, each about 1½ inches (4 cm) long. Sew them together in pairs to make five crosses.* Enjoy your game of tic tac toe!

Handy Holders

Try stitching felt pockets to create a useful wall hanger for storing all your stuff.

1. *Find or cut some rectangles of colorful felt.*

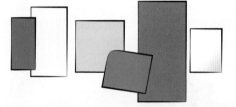

2. *Fold up a rectangle to leave a flap at the top, like this, and pin it in place.*

3. *Choose a bright thread that stands out against the felt, and sew up the two sides to make a pocket. Use running stitch, backstitch, or up-and-over stitch.*

Thick, doubled thread stands out better.

4. *When you've made a few pockets, tack them to a cork board.*

Add stitches on the front of the pockets for decoration.

Cool Creatures

Once you've tried sewing with felt, you can cut more complicated shapes and create amazing animal toys. Experiment with the designs on this page, and then invent more of your own!

Body Basics

To make animal characters, you first need a body template. Draw an oval, about 3 inches (8 cm) long, on paper or card stock and cut it out.

Draw around your template twice onto felt. Try starting with brown felt to make a bear. Cut out the shapes.

Dark pencil should show up, or use ballpoint pen–but then turn the felt piece over, so pen marks are on the back.

Cut small shapes for ears, four paws, and a circle of white felt for the bear's muzzle.

Did You Know?

The art of decorating fabric using stitches and other, smaller pieces of fabric or decorations is called appliqué.

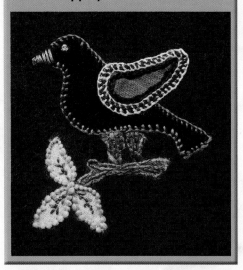

Start Sewing

Now make your bear!

1. *First, sew the white muzzle onto one of the body ovals with small, neat running stitches in white thread.*

2. *Using a doubled black thread, make lots of little stitches to create eyes and a nose. Make a mouth with backstitch.*

3. Put the two body ovals together and sew along the edges with brown running stitch. When you come to places where an ear or paw should go, sandwich them between the ovals and stitch them, too.

Don't go all the way around–leave a gap.

4. Use your fingertips to gently push a little stuffing inside to pad out your bear.

5. Finally, finish sewing around the edge.

More Ideas

Now make more animals, using the same basic design: two body ovals plus extra paws, legs, tails, or wings! Remember to stitch details on the face or body before sewing the ovals together. Soon, you could have a whole zoo of furry animals!

Cool Idea

Turn felt animals into finger puppets by keeping the base unstitched and leaving out the stuffing. Unstuffed animals also make great bookmarks.

The creatures you make may depend on the colors of felt you have.

Buttons and Beads

Why not attach other decorations to fabric, such as buttons and beads? They're easy to sew on with just a few stitches, as long as your needle is thin enough to go through the holes.

Button Badges

Make artsy badges by layering different colored felt shapes, then adding a bright button on top. Sew it all together with thick thread in an 'x' through the button holes. Sew a small strip of felt to the back with a safety pin in the middle, and your badge is ready.

Make sure the safety pin is positioned to open outwards, so you can pin it on.

Cool Idea

Look in thrift stores for clothes with interesting or unusual buttons. They may be a lot cheaper than buying a new set of buttons.

Most buttons are plastic, but some are made of metal, wood, or shell. Instead of holes, some have a molded loop on the back called a shank.

Cool Key Rings

Make a personalized key ring using a plain metal key ring, felt, thread and extra decorations. Choose buttons or beads to design funny faces, patterns, or your initials.

1. Draw around a circular object, such as a cookie cutter, on felt. Draw another circle about an inch (2.5 cm) beneath, and draw lines to connect the two, like this.

These go back to back to make up the two halves of your key ring.

2. Cut out the shape and decorate each circle. The section of circle connected to the central strip will be the top of each.

3. Feed one felt circle through a metal key ring. Sew the circles together with an up-and-over stitch. Add a little stuffing before sewing the last bit.

Use a double thread and sew on each bead with several stitches to make sure it's firmly fixed.

Did You Know?

Traditional Chinese buttons are made of knotted strings and are called frogs.

Bling a Bag

You can sew decorations directly on to clothes or other fabrics. Why not find a plain canvas bag, cover it in bright buttons, beads, and thin strips of ribbon, and give it to your mom or grandma as a gift?

Sock Puppets

Sock puppets are fun to make, and they look better and last longer if they're sewn rather than held together with glue. Find a few old, clean socks and some spare buttons. Then design a cast of crazy characters.

Funny Faces

1. *Put your sock on a hand, heel on top, and mark pen dots where you want the eyes to go.*

2. *Sew on two large buttons, tying the thread inside the sock. You may need to roll up the open end to reach inside.*

3. *Cut a red felt oval to sew underneath the toe end of the sock, and make your character's mouth. Add a pink tongue.*

4. *Sew two small beads to the tip of the toe for nostrils.*

Adding Extras

Now add more features to give your puppet personality!

For hair, loop a long length of yarn together...

...then sew it in place with more yarn of the same color. Make sure it covers the heel of the sock.

Add glasses made from a pipe cleaner, jewelry from beads threaded on elastic, or sew on a bow tie, scarf, or hair ribbon. Use your imagination!

Animal Ears

There are several ways of making animal ears. One method is to sew on two pieces of felt to make long, floppy dog ears, like this.

Or, try turning the sock inside out and snip the heel down the middle. Use an up-and-over stitch to sew the cut edges together. Turn the sock the right way out, and two little ears will poke up. Stuff them to make them stand up well.

Cool Idea

Take funny photos of your sock puppets, and send them to friends to make them smile.

It's easy to rip out stitching and remove or adjust features that aren't in quite the right place. Don't stop until you're happy with your creation!

Did You Know?

A wrestler named Mick Foley wore a sock puppet on his hand during fights and used it to perform wrestling moves on his opponents!

Beautiful Bags

Drawstring bags are great sewing projects. They're also useful for storing your stuff, whether you need a secret container for precious things, or a spacious tote bag to cart around your swimming gear!

Speedy Felt Bag

Use this soft bag as a money pouch, or give it away as a stylish gift bag. You can vary the size to make a bigger or taller bag.

1. *Cut a rectangle of felt and fold it double.*

2. *Sew up each long side. Use backstitch to hold the **seams** together firmly.*

3. *Turn the bag inside out. Use thick thread to sew large running stitches around the bag, near the top. Start at the front, and don't pull the thread all the way through.*

4. *Remove the needle, and cut the two dangling ends of thread to the same length. Pull to tighten them, and tie them in a bow.*

Did You Know?

Drawstring bags and pouches have been used to carry money since ancient times.

Give your bag extra style by adding beads to the ends of the thread.

Pillow Bags

Pillowcases are practically bags already—all you need to do is add a drawstring. Here's how.

1. *Find an old pillowcase and turn it inside out.*

2. *Use small, sharp scissors (or a **seam ripper**) to snip the stitches from the top of a side seam. Stop when you've made a 2 inch (5 cm) split.*

5 cm

Don't snip the fabric!

3. *Fold down the top of the pillowcase 1 inch (2.5 cm), level with the end of the split. Pin in place.*

One side will be double thickness because of the inner flap.

4. *Stitch all the way around the pillowcase with small, neat running stitches. This creates a tube (called a casing) for the drawstring to go through.*

This will be the inside of your bag, so make sure you tie knots on this side.

5. *Turn the pillowcase right side out. Find a long piece of cord, string, ribbon, or braid. Attach a large safety pin to the end and feed it through the casing.*

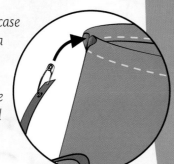

6. *Remove the safety pin. Your drawstring bag is ready to fill!*

Cool Idea
Choose a patterned pillowcase, or add lines of stitching, buttons, or beads to liven up a plain one.

Clothes Craft

You can transform more than just pillowcases. Here are some great ways of recycling your old clothes into cool stuff for your bedroom.

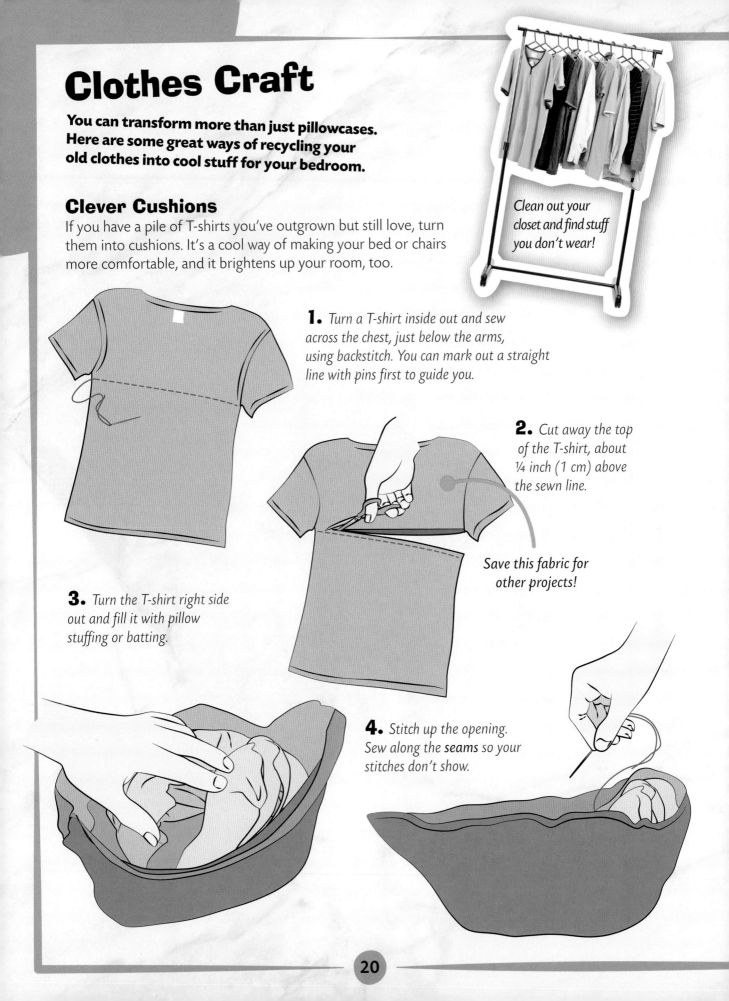

Clean out your closet and find stuff you don't wear!

Clever Cushions

If you have a pile of T-shirts you've outgrown but still love, turn them into cushions. It's a cool way of making your bed or chairs more comfortable, and it brightens up your room, too.

1. Turn a T-shirt inside out and sew across the chest, just below the arms, using backstitch. You can mark out a straight line with pins first to guide you.

2. Cut away the top of the T-shirt, about ¼ inch (1 cm) above the sewn line.

Save this fabric for other projects!

3. Turn the T-shirt right side out and fill it with pillow stuffing or batting.

4. Stitch up the opening. Sew along the **seams** so your stitches don't show.

Keep your T-shirt cushion simple, like this one, or sew on buttons and other decorations.

Secret Sewing

Do you need a place to hide secret notes, keys, or money from nosy brothers or sisters? Find something you don't wear any more, preferably with an inner lining, and sew a felt pocket to the lining. The stitches won't show, and no one will know the pocket is there!

Cool Idea

Make a felt pocket like those on page 11 and sew the flap around a coat hanger. Cover it with clothes, and you have a secret compartment!

Did You Know?

You can buy socks and even underwear with secret zip compartments for storing valuables!

Another good spot is inside a tie. Use small, sharp scissors to rip the seam a little bit...

... and then sew in a small pocket into the inner lining. Sew a small **snap** to each side of the tie seam to close it, so no one will see it's not sewn.

Bath-Time Treats

Terrycloth is a soft, woven fabric used for making towels and washcloths. It's ideal for sewing this hooded towel and matching mitt. They make great gifts for your friends and family, or keep them for yourself!

Cozy Hoodie

To make this easy hooded towel, you need one big bath towel and one hand towel.

1. *Cut the hand towel in half. Put one half aside for making the bath mitt later.*

2. *Lay the bath towel on the floor, underside up. Position half of the hand towel at the top, in the middle, also with the underside facing up. Pin the edges together.*

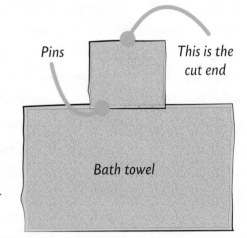

Pins

This is the cut end

Bath towel

3. *Stitch the edges together using backstitch.*

4. *Turn over the towels, and fold them in half, like this. Pin the cut end of the hand towel together about 1 inch (2.5 cm) from the top and sew it up with backstitch.*

Pin and sew this edge 1 inch (2.5 cm) from the top.

5. *Turn your hood the right way out, and your towel is finished!*

Did You Know?

The world's most expensive bath towels are made from soft, plush Egyptian cotton and cost about $1,300 each!

*Decorate your mitt by sewing colorful ribbon or **rickrack** neatly around it.*

Easy Mitt

Making a bath mitt with the other half of the hand towel is even simpler.

1. *Make a template. Sketch a round-ended rectangle on scrap paper, like this. It should be bigger than your hand (or the hand of the person who'll be using the mitt).*

2. *Cut out the template and pin it on the towel, lining up the bottom edges.*

3. *Cut around the template, leaving at least ¼ inch (1 cm) extra all the way around.*

4. *Make a second mitt shape in the same way, and pin the two together, about ¼ inch (1 cm) from the edge. Make sure the undersides of the towel shapes are facing outwards.*

5. *Sew the shapes together and remove all the pins. Turn your finished mitt the right way out.*

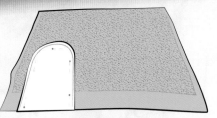

Cool Idea

Fill a bath mitt with fancy soaps to make a really thoughtful gift for someone special.

Get Decorating!

It's easy to sew great decorations for parties and celebrations. Why not adapt the animal designs from pages 12 and 13 to make Easter eggs, Halloween pumpkins, or Christmas gingerbread men? Here are some more decoration ideas.

Great Garlands

Make simple garlands from felt shapes and hang them from curtain rails and lampshades, or loop them around the room in long strings.

1. *Decide on a shape and cut out card templates. Circles, stars, and diamonds work well. Draw around the templates on felt, and cut out the shapes.*

2. *Lay the shapes in a line, and sew them together with running stitch. Don't pull the thread all the way through— leave a long tail at each end for hanging your garland.*

3. *Tie a neat knot below the last shape, and your decoration is ready to hang.*

 Cool Idea

Sew layers of felt shapes together, and thread small craft pompoms in between to make your garlands really eye-catching.

Fun Flags

Strings of flags called bunting are perfect for indoor or outdoor parties, or just for brightening up your bedroom. Make them using old shirts, sheets, or scraps of patterned fabric.

1. Draw a triangle template on card. Add a flap at the top and cut it out.

Draw around the template on the underside of the material, so the pen marks won't show.

2. Cut triangles from your material using the template.

3. Fold the flap of each triangle over a long strip of thin ribbon, pin them in place, and sew along the ribbon with running stitch.

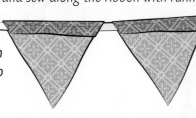

Sew through both layers of fabric, so it's firmly fixed.

4. Leave some ribbon at each end for tying or taping up your bunting.

Did You Know?

Dressmaking scissors called **pinking shears** give material a zigzag edge and keep it from fraying so easily. Why not use a pair to make bunting?

Clever Cards

Use your sewing skills to create special, home-made cards. Stitch patterns on felt, and stick the fabric on colorful cardstock using **PVA glue**. Or forget the fabric altogether, and sew directly onto the card!

Cool Idea

For unique party invitations or gift tags, make holes with a hole punch around rectangles of cardstock, then thread ribbon in and out of the holes.

Prick and Stitch

Use this prick and stitch method for sewing on cardstock. Don't make the holes too close together, or the card may tear.

1. *Draw a simple picture, pattern, or letter on the back of a piece of cardstock.*

2. *Place the cardstock on an old notepad or pile of magazines. Use a thick, blunt darning needle to prick evenly-spaced holes around the shape. Press hard.*

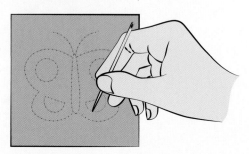

The holes don't need to go all the way through the card. They will show up as bumps on the other side.

3. *Turn over the card and sew around your shape, using the bumps to guide your needle. Work slowly and carefully to avoid bending or tearing the card.*

As you finish each color, cut the thread at the back and tape down the end.

4. *Cut out your finished design and **mount** it on a larger piece of folded cardstock.*

Thread a few small beads onto stitches to add extra texture.

Starbursts

Now try this really cool card-sewing trick.

1. Draw a circle on cardstock and prick holes around it. Make sure there are an even number of holes.

2. Turn over the card. Pull thread up through one hole and down the hole directly opposite. Count the holes on either side to be sure it's the right hole.

Use a long piece of thread.

3. Come up at the hole to the left of the one you just went down, and take the thread across the circle again, going down at the hole on the right of the first.

4. Keep going like this until you've been through each hole. Cut the thread at the back and tape down the end.

Make lots of similar shapes to create a fantastic starburst pattern.

Did You Know?

*Many **scrapbook** makers use thread to stitch fancy borders around pages or sew on fabric decorations called embellishments.*

Amazing Art

Don't throw away scraps of fabric, extra buttons, bits of thread, and odd lengths of ribbon. Keep them in a big box and use them to create fantastic pieces of art.

Ribbon Stripes

Here's an easy idea to start with. Find a photo frame and cut a piece of felt to fit inside it. Arrange strips of ribbon across the felt in a criss-cross pattern.

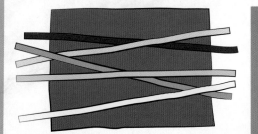

Use a plain frame in a contrasting color to make your pattern stand out.

Take a photo of the strips so you remember the arrangement, then move them off the felt. Sew them on, one by one, using running stitch. Choose thread that matches each ribbon, and make the stitches on the top very small, so they're not obvious.

Frame your stripy picture and display it!

Cool Idea

Ask an adult to iron any ribbons or scraps of material before you use them. They'll lie flatter on the felt and be easier to sew.

Cool Collages

A great way of using up leftovers is to create a big, sewn **collage**. Look at the colors and textures of your fabric scraps to give you ideas, then sketch out a scene on paper.

Don't make your design too complicated. You can always add extra details later.

Start with a big piece of felt for the background, and sew on smaller pieces of fabric to build up the picture. Use layers to create depth, and add ribbon, lace, buttons, and beads for fine details. You could even sew on extras such as feathers, plastic gems, and sequins.

Glossary

collage
A collection of materials, artistically arranged and fixed in place, either by sewing or gluing.

cross-stitch
A type of embroidery in which blocks of many small "x"-shaped stitches build up pictures and patterns.

darning
A method of mending holes or worn areas, for example in socks, by weaving thread in and out of the fabric.

embroidery
The craft of decorating fabric using different stitches made with a needle and thread.

felt
Fabric made from pressed, matted wool.

fray
To unravel into loose threads at the edges.

mount
To fix something in place on a background to display it.

pinking shears
Scissors with blades that are shaped to make a serrated edge.

PVA glue
A strong, water-based glue, also known as white craft glue. PVA stands for polyvinyl acetate, which is a rubbery plastic substance.

rickrack

rickrack
Flat, narrow, cotton braid, woven in a wavy, zigzag shape.

scrapbook
A decorated album that may be filled with photos, drawings, notes, and other personal details or keepsakes.

seam
The edge where two pieces of fabric have been sewn together.

seam ripper
A small tool with a forked handle, used for lifting and cutting through stitches to rip them.

snap
A pair of small metal or plastic disks that snap together and pull apart.

threader
A small device for helping to thread a needle. Threaders are usually made of thin, flimsy metal, so use them carefully.

seam ripper

Websites

Holiday Crafts and Creations
www.holiday-crafts-and-creations.com/craft-tips.html
Find clear instructions and photos to help you learn basic stitches.

The Crafty Crow
www.thecraftycrow.net/sewing-stitchery
Discover all kinds of simple sewing projects for beginners.

Sewing Crafts
tlc.howstuffworks.com/family/sewing-crafts.htm
Have fun making lots of different sewing projects.

Fun Felt Crafts for Kids
www.bhg.com/crafts/kids/rainy-day/kids-felt-crafts
Practice your sewing skills with these fun felt crafts.

Index

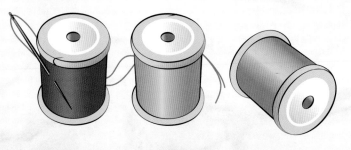